W9-CSO-341

DISCARD

Dedicated to
my grandchildren...
Ruth Bell
Sophia Frances
Anne Riggin
...and yours

*Anne Graham Lotz*

Dedicated to J. D. B.

*Laura J. Bryant*

DISCARD

# Dear Reader,

Thank you for choosing this book to read to a child. I pray that it will help to plant the seeds of genuine faith in a small heart. My desire is that this little book will help you be intentional about passing genuine faith in Jesus to the children you read it to.

I am asked repeatedly how my parents were able to pass on to me their faith in Jesus. Although there are several answers to that question, one underlying fact is that my parents were intentional about it. They did not leave the instruction of biblical truth to the pastor or Sunday school teacher or visiting evangelist to carry out. They did not assume that just because I was their child I would somehow "catch faith" like a contagious disease. They themselves, along with my maternal grandparents, accepted the privilege and the responsibility of teaching me God's Word in a way that was personal, relevant, and easy to understand. Then I had to choose to respond and make their faith my own, which I did as a young girl.

I am now seeking to help my daughter pass on our faith to my own three young granddaughters. They have already gone through the loss of my beloved mother—their great-grandmother—Ruth Bell Graham. I have found that helping my granddaughters to focus beyond the grave has helped ease their pain, comfort their fears, enlarge their faith, and has given us opportunity to talk about Heaven. As a result, I have written this book for them, and for you.

If you sense that your child sincerely wants to accept Jesus' invitation to be welcomed into Heaven, please take the opportunity seriously. My granddaughters prayed a prayer similar to the one at the end of this book at just under three years of age. Although they didn't understand everything, they understood enough to confess their sin and ask Jesus to forgive them and come into their hearts. I have since seen evidence that He answered their prayer and does indeed live within them … and therefore I am assured that Heaven is their home too.

For His glory,

# Anne Graham Lotz

Look closely at the pictures and see if you can find the angels.

J236.24
LOT

ZONDERKIDZ

*Heaven, God's Promise for Me*
Copyright © 2011 by Anne Graham Lotz
Illustrations © 2011 by Laura J. Bryant

Requests for information should be addressed to:
*Zonderkidz, Grand Rapids, Michigan 49530*

Library of Congress Cataloging-in-Publication Data

Lotz, Anne Graham, 1948-
    Heaven, God's promise for me / by Anne Graham Lotz; illustrated by Laura J.
Bryant.
        p. cm.
    ISBN  978-0-310-71601-3 (hardcover)
    [1. Heaven—Christianity—Juvenile literature. I. Bryant, Laura J. II. Heaven, God's
Promise for Me.
    BT849.L68 2011
    236'.24—dc22
                                          2009014235

Scriptures taken from the Holy Bible, *New International Reader's Version®, NIrV®.*
Copyright© 1995, 1996, 1998 by Biblica, Inc.™ Used by permission of Zondervan. All
rights reserved worldwide.

Any Internet addresses (websites, blogs, etc.) and telephone numbers printed in
this book are offered as a resource. They are not intended in any way to be or imply
an endorsement by Zondervan, nor does Zondervan vouch for the content of these
sites and numbers for the life of this book.

All rights reserved. No part of this publication may be reproduced, stored in a re-
trieval system, or transmitted in any form or by any means—electronic, mechanical,
photocopy, recording, or any other—except for brief quotations in printed reviews,
without the prior permission of the publisher.

Published in association with the literary agency of Alive Communications, Inc.,
7680 Goddard Street, Suite 200, Colorado Springs, CO 80920, www.alivecom-
munications.com

Zonderkidz is a trademark of Zondervan.

*Editor: Barbara Herndon*
*Art direction and design: Cindy Davis*

*Printed in China*

11 12 13 14 /LPC/ 10 9 8 7 6 5 4 3 2 1

MARCH 2012

# Heaven

## God's Promise for Me

story by
### Anne Graham Lotz
pictures by
### Laura J. Bryant

CARLSBAD
CITY LIBRARY
Carlsbad, CA
92011

ZONDERkidz

ZONDERVAN.com/
AUTHORTRACKER
*follow your favorite authors*

I have a little brother,
He's as cute as he can be.
We do everything together,
And he always looks up to me.

We couldn't fall asleep last week
When we went to bed.
We had so many questions,
Thoughts were swirling in our heads.

We wondered when our Granny died,
Where did she really go?
It's lonely here without her,
And we just miss her so!

Then we whispered a little prayer
That only God could hear.
*Give us some answers, please.*
*We want to feel You near.*

In the quietness of the night,
This is what we heard.
This is what God said to us
Right from His holy Word.

"Don't let your hearts be troubled.
There's nothing you should fear.
In My home that I call Heaven,
Our loved ones are always near."

He said His home is a great big house
With lots of rooms and space,
Filled with gifts and laughter and love…
With smiles on every face.

Jesus, His Son, is preparing a place
With treasures from above—
Our favorite foods and colors
And the special people we love.

Whatever makes us happy,
Whatever makes us glad,
We'll find it all in heaven
Where no one will be sad.

If there are tears on your face
When you arrive on that day,
Jesus Himself
Will wipe them away.

Inside there is no crying.
Inside there is no pain.
Inside there are no bad people.
You'll never be lonely again.

Your home in Heaven is so wonderful.
It's much more than you can dream.
There will be no sickness or sadness,
And everything will be clean.

There will be no more crutches
Or hospital stays.
There will be no more hunger...
He will take it away.

You will walk and run.
You will play and sing.
You will have many friends.
Heaven will never be boring.

You will be safe,
And you will be free.
Nothing will hurt you.
Not even a bee!

You can pet a lion.

You can swim
with a shark.

You can fly with an eagle.
And it will never get dark.

The Light is always on
Because Jesus is waiting for you.
The very best part of Heaven
Is that He's going to be there too.

Your heavenly home is beautiful.
The glassy streets are gold.
The Light of Jesus comes shining through...
And there's nothing at all that is old.

The walls are so strong.
The walls are so wide.
Twenty chariots could fit on top ...
And still race side by side!

The ground has layers of jewels.
But the most beautiful gems of all
Are the great big gates of pearl
That hang in the city wall.

Each gate is a single pearl
Made from a grain of sand
By oysters that suffered greatly
To teach us about God's plan.

Because God's plan comes from His heart,
He sent Jesus to suffer and die.
Then God raised Him up from death and the grave
To open those pearly gates wide.

Jesus wants His home to be yours
And invites you to live there forever.
He wants to know you are coming.
You must tell Him yourself … not another.

Make sure that *you* respond.
Say yes to His invitation.
Then look forward with lots of excitement
To an out-of-this-world destination!

Do you want to know how to get there?
Do you want to know the way?
Jesus said, "If you come through Me,
You'll be welcomed in Heaven one day!"

So, *please* ... put your trust in Jesus.
Ask Him to forgive your sin.
Invite Him to live in your heart,
So one day you'll live with Him ...

# Forever!

God had answered our questions
As we lay there on our bed.
Our hearts were filled with peace
As His Word then filled our heads.

So... we put our trust in Jesus.
We asked Him to forgive our sin.
We invited Him to live in our hearts,
And know one day we'll live with Him!

Getting to Heaven is not hard.
You can actually go there with ease.
You don't even have to be perfect.
You just need to say, "Jesus … please."

If you want Heaven to be your home,
If you're quite sure you want to go,
Pray this little prayer we prayed
And in your heart you will know.

Dear Jesus,
I want to go to Heaven one day.
I'm sorry for my sin.
I believe You died on the Cross for me.
Please wash me clean within.

I believe You rose up from the grave.
You're alive in Heaven today.
I invite You to come into my heart.
I give You my life for always.

Now I know that when I die
I won't be afraid.
You are my heavenly Father.
And I'm going to the House You made.

Amen.

*After you pray this prayer, look for the special invitation*
*in the back of this book with your RSVP to Jesus.*

Do not let your hearts be troubled
Trust in God.  Trust in me also:
There are many rooms in my Father's house...
I will come back. And I will take you to be with me.
Then you will also be where I am.

— John 14:1-3

Here are some questions
to help you talk
about Heaven and the
ideas in this book.

What is Heaven? Where is it?

Where does Jesus live now?

Who lives in Heaven with Jesus?

What makes you happy? What makes you sad?

What makes you afraid?

Will there be anything that scares you in Heaven?

What are some of your favorite things (food, color, animal)?

Do you think Jesus will have your favorite things in Heaven? Why?

What would you like to do in Heaven that you can't do right now?

What sickness or hurts have you had?

Is there someone you love who is sick or hurt?

Will there be hurts in Heaven?

When you get to Heaven, what will you be glad is *not* there?

What will you be glad *is* there?

What do you like most about Heaven?

Is it hard to get to Heaven?

Will you be welcomed in Heaven? Why?

How long will you live in Heaven?

Is there enough room in Heaven for those who want to go?

Who do you want to go to Heaven with you?

Have you invited Jesus to come into your heart?

Would you share this book with your friends
 so they can know that heaven is for them too?

# Did You Know?

Did you know that everything you just read about Heaven is the truth? It is not imagination or fantasy. It is promised in God's Word. The following Scripture references are given to reassure you that what you have read is an application of God's Word as it is found primarily in John 14:1–6 and Revelation 21:1–27.

Isaiah 11:6–9

John 1:12

John 3:16

John 14:1–6

John 20:31

Romans 10:9–13

1 Corinthians 2:9

Revelation 19:9

Revelation 21:1–5, 14–27

Revelation 22:1–2, 5